PAISLEY Since the War

by

Donald Malcolm

To all the usual suspects, Bob Preston, Alan Lacey, Andy Robertson and Peter Westwood for many enjoyal

An early 1950s montage of local schools. Of the four, only the Grammar, with extensions, still exists.
The demolition of Camphill (1888–1969) and Ferguslie/Craigielea (1876–1978) deprived the town of two architectural treasures.

© Donald Malcolm 2000
First published in the United Kingdom, 2000,
by Stenlake Publishing
Telephone / Fax: 01290 551122

ISBN 1 84033 131 3

ACKNOWLEDGEMENTS

Derek Malcolm (proof-reading), Bill Baillie, Tom Baillie, Alex B. Greer, Carl Neilson, Sydney Rennie, Andy Robertson and Mr Hamilton, Local Government Library, County Buildings. Special thanks to David A. Roberts, Photographic Archivist, Museum and Art Galleries, Renfrewshire Council and Hugh Ferguson Gibson for the provision of many of the pieces used in this book. And finally to David Rowand, FSA (Scotland) whose unrivalled knowledge of the history of Paisley was of inestimable value.

PICTURE CREDITS

Inside front cover, Andrew Robertson. 4 (Wallneuk football team), Sydney Rennie. 9, Carl Neilson. 12 (Stewart Granger) and 39, Alex. B. Greer. 30, Bill Baillie. Front cover, back cover, 2, 12, 13, 18, 19, 20, 26, 37, 38, Hugh Ferguson Gibson. 11, 21, 22, 23, 24, 25, 27, 30 (organ), 32, 33, 34, 35, 44–45, 46, 47, Museum and Art Galleries, Renfrewshire Council. 28, Philip G. Doughty, photographer. Other images, Donald Malcolm.

FURTHER READING

The books listed below were used by the author during his research. None of them are available from Stenlake Publishing. Those interested in finding out more are advised to contact their local bookshop or reference library.

Brotchie, A. W. and Grieves, R. L., *Paisley's Trams and Buses*, two volumes: *Eighties to Twenties* (1986), *Twenties to Eighties* (1988), NB Traction, Dundee.

Clark, Sylvia, *Paisley: A History*, Mainstream Publishing, 1988.

McCarthy, Mary, *A Social Geography of Paisley*, Paisley Public Library, 1969.

Reilly, Valerie, *Paisley in Old Picture Postcards*, European Library, 1983.

Rowand, David FSA (Scotland), *Golden Threads*, Paisley Daily Express, 1999.

Rowand, David, *A Pictorial History of Paisley*, Alloway Press, 1993.

Walker, Frank Arneil, *The South Clyde Estuary*, Scottish Academic Press, 1968, for the Royal Incorporation of Architects in Scotland.

ALSO AVAILABLE FROM STENLAKE PUBLISHING

The following books about Paisley, also by Donald Malcolm, are available direct from the publisher or from bookshops:

Yesterday's Paisley
Coal Flowers: Memories of a Paisley Childhood
The Paisley Rocketeers

FOREWORD

This book is a miscellany, covering many subjects. It includes people, places, personalities, protests, parades, plays, provosts, politics and poets. The pictures are funny, amusing, humorous, industrious, serious, dramatic. They reflect a town recovering from the trauma of global war. Some of the subjects are undated or only approximately dated, but they don't lose any of their impact because of that. The woman protester at the railings will always be dramatic. In a way, this is a who-are-you, where-are-you kind of a book, intended to convey the richness and variety that was post-war Paisley. If you open it at a page and exclaim 'Heavens, it's me!' or 'I know that person' (or place or occasion), so much the better. Previous Paisley books have brought letters from faraway corners of the world, so let's hear from you.

Donald Malcolm
28 September 2000

Paisley has a long association with drama groups, such as the Paisley Players and the Grammar School group. This picture shows the cast of the Brown and Polson Players, in a play staged in February 1959. Their plays were usually performed in the B&P Recreation Club, on the opposite side of Braids Road from the main factory (which has now been converted into flats). I recognise most of the cast, but can name only a few: Louis Williams (standing far left), George Stubbs (standing right – an old sporting chum of mine), Helen Dickie (the maid, sitting) and Ingrid Armour (right, my sister-in-law). On Saturday 14 February 1959, the SCDA one-act play Preliminary Festival was held in the West School hall, and the picture may have been taken there.

It's always an event when a team other than Rangers or Celtic win the Scottish Cup. St Mirren had their first moment of glory in 1926 and had to wait until 1959 for their second success, when they beat Aberdeen 3–1 at Hampden Park before a capacity crowd. I returned from the game, met my wife, Rita, with our first son, Gordon, in – appropriately – his black and white pram and joined the thousands who welcomed the team with the cup on the balcony of the Municipal Buildings in County Square. There was a palpable air of excitement and strangers spoke to each other, proud of a fine sporting achievement. This picture shows the winning team.

Back row: E. McGarvie (trainer), J. Wilson, G. Baker, D. Walker, J. Neilson, J. McGugan, T. Leishman.
Front row: J. Rodger, T. Bryceland, D. Lapsley, T. Gemmell, A. Miller.

The team in 1956–1957. A new stand has since blocked the view of the tenements.

Here's the Wallneuk Mission team photographed *c*.1952 at the racecourse, and not a foreign player in sight (no one from Johnstone or Barrhead, that is). Sydney Rennie, whose picture this is, commented in his letter that 'We played in blue shirts and white shorts (when available)'. None of this changing the strips twice a year and fleecing our three supporters. I do recall that after receiving a windfall we were kitted out in green and white hooped jerseys and our results began to improve. However, as a warning against excessive hubris, the day the McNaughton brothers sailed for Canada, we were hammered 8–0.

Back row: T. Fisher, A. N. Other (I recognise him), W. Vessey, S. Rennie, D. Malcolm, G. Stubbs.
Front row: R. Anderson, W. McNaughton, C. Johnson, J. McNaughton, T. Anderson.

Tennis aces? Who knows, we might have been. As soon as the tennis season started, many youngsters headed for the public courts. Our chosen venue was at Braids Road, and at the end of the first day, most of the bright enthusiasts would limp stiffly off court, the penalty for overdoing things. Britain's lack of success at higher levels can be traced back to the fact that there was little, if any, coaching of players, certainly not at public level. Our prize player was Alex McCulloch. The line-up here is:

Back row: N. Mack, D. Malcolm, R. Hunter(?), G. Stubbs.
Front row: N. Barr, W. Gould, W. Pirie, A. Castles.

(The names were supplied by Sydney Rennie, an old friend and a tennis and football partner.)

The Royal Highland Show, St James'
Racecourse, 1950. Paisley first hosted the
show in 1913 and it was a great success.
The 1950 event was on a much larger
scale. The *Gazette* of 24 June reported that
'Most of those who had taken ground
space struck a bright note with their
pavilions – without being garish – and it
was a case of flowers everywhere, while
flags, streamers and banners fluttered
aloft'. The crowds certainly turned out
in their thousands. Here are two excellent
postcards of the event. No. 991 was the
winning Shetland mare, Harviestoun
Princess, and her foal, owned by J. E. Kerr
of Harviestoun, Dollar.

Just after the War, Canada was the unrivalled exponent of ice hockey, with great teams such as the Toronto Maple Leafs and the Montreal Canadiens battling it out with four American teams for the prestigious Stanley Cup. The game was quickly established in Scotland and England, and our team was the Paisley Pirates. I was a keen supporter and attended regularly at East Lane. Paisley stars did much to encourage young players. One of the most talented team-members was Rhael Savard, seen here. Savard was a prolific scorer and in a game at Dundee, when the Tigers were mauled by 14–8, he rifled in 10 or 11 goals. These days, the Pirates haven't been doing so well. An old school chum of mine, Ian Burnie, is sitting on the barrier, at the left of the picture.

Board of Management for Paisley and District Hospitals.

Phone—
PAISLEY **4248/4249**

Barshaw Maternity Hospital

VISITING HOURS

Wednesday, Saturday, and Sunday, 2 to 3 p.m.

Name, *Donald Malcolm*

Address, *42 Garry Dr*

NOTE.—This Card must be produced when inquiring at Hospital, and if the Patient's condition, in the opinion of the Medical Officer, permits, two Visitors are allowed, one at a time. Children under 16 years of age not admitted.

250. 7. 58 A.G. 4465

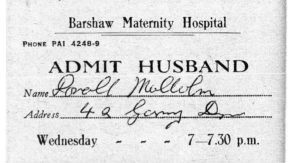

Barshaw Maternity Hospital

PHONE PAI **4248-9**

ADMIT HUSBAND

Name *Donald Malcolm*

Address *42 Garry Dr*

Wednesday - - - 7—7.30 p.m.

Sometimes more-so than a photograph, a ticket or other keepsake at the back of a drawer can bring back special memories. How many men reading this kept their admission card for the maternity hospital? ADMIT HUSBAND: you can't get any more unequivocal than that. And the strict visiting conditions make odd reading today: 'two visitors are allowed, one at a time. Children under 16 years of age not admitted'. Barshaw mansion house, built by Robert Smith, was the home of Glasgow merchant James Arthur and his wife. In its long existence, the building has been a military hospital, a maternity unit (our elder son was born there in 1958), a geriatric unit and in 1999 was converted into luxury flats.

MANSION HOUSE BARSHAW PARK, PAISLEY

38

Carl Neilson was fifteen when he joined the GPO at County Square as a junior postman. Previously this grade was known as telegraph boy, and the uniform included a pillbox hat. At the changeover, c.1949, a postman-type cap became the regulation headgear. In this photograph Carl is tootling down the High Street, towards the Cross, in the early 1950s. Junior postmen delivered telegrams (and Express Letters) and would take a reply of up to nine words free of charge. They covered a wide area, travelling to places such as the RNAS at Abbotsinch, Georgetown munitions factory (sometimes by train), up the Braes to the Peesweep (with Express Letters only) and Ralston and Elderslie. Capes, leggings and boots were supplied during the winter. Carl joked that runs would only be cancelled if the snow was ten feet deep. Tokens for trams and trains were supplied. When he retired after 40 years' service, Carl was Area Delivery Manager, Paisley.

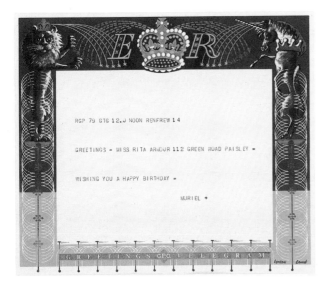

This is an example of the special type of greetings telegram that Carl would have delivered. It was postmarked at Paisley on 25 July 1953, my wife's 21st birthday.

5th year pupils, Camphill Secondary School, 1948–1949. Most of us have a school photograph tucked away somewhere, and looking at them is a journey back in time. Occasionally I still bump into an old school friend. I met one called Thomas Wilson – known as Tote for an obvious reason – in the Paisley Abbey bookshop in 1998; I hadn't seen him since 1949 and yet he only lives about three miles away. Another one, Margaret Graham, knew me. I couldn't recall her name but, strangely, I recognised her eyes. Tom is fourth left in the front row of boys and Margaret is fourth left in the front row.

This picture of a group of pupils at Paisley Grammar dates from *c.*1952, but, unfortunately, the class wasn't noted. It looks about 4th year level. The picture was donated to the museum by Mr Bernard Butcher, now of Derby, whose wife is in the group.

Here is Scotland's Queen of Song, Moira Anderson, in Paisley promoting her latest LP, probably in the early 1960s. On another visit to the town she had less to smile about. The occasion was a concert in the Town Hall, with Peter Morrison and Iain Sutherland (who, incidentally, forgot which tune was supposed to be coming next at one point). Moira was singing when someone shouted out that he couldn't hear. It wasn't meant as a heckle and like the professional that she was, Moira had a word with him and carried on singing. From my seat, I could hear clearly and I'm hard of hearing. I'll bet that she didn't forget that visit in a hurry.

Under the old Hollywood star system, when the lives of actors and actresses under contract were organised from dawn till dusk, many of the arranged appearances were not of their choice. But the selection of cover girl for *The News Reel* (the magazine of J. & P. Coats) in 1948 must have been one of the more pleasant ones for Stewart Granger. The winner was Lena McCurry, Miss Glasgow. This picture shows the actor (whose real name was James Stewart – sound familiar?) with the winner's photograph.

The smiling man was James Wallace of Scotia Recording Studios, a producer of Scottish albums. He's seen here with two Alec Finlay recordings and a photograph of Finlay and Harry Lauder, who signed the picture 'To Jean Wallace, from Harry Lauder and Alec Finlay. Harry says "She's my Bonnie, Bonnie Jean" '.

Someone at the postcard publishers Valentines – probably a staff photographer – was alert to historical recording and sales potential when he spotted the change in this part of the Paisley landscape. This card shows the Bladda fever hospital, also known as the Bridge Street Hospital, at the bottom left of the 1935 panorama. The splendid building to the left of the billboard was The Lighthouse public house.

This photograph, taken from virtually the same angle (but note the inclusion of the white buildings at the right) and time of day – between 2.20 and 2.45 – shows that the hospital has been demolished and the site cleared. This particular postcard was used in July 1947, although David Rowand dates it to 1938 in his *Pictorial History of Paisley*. As I related in *Yesterday's Paisley*: 'I was incarcerated there (with measles I think). Then children's parents were not allowed in, of course, and they used to congregate in the street below, while we talked to them out of the windows!'

The High Street was Paisley's main artery. Buildings, shopfronts and vehicles are all shown to fine effect as a background to bustling pedestrians in this lively postcard view, looking east along the street. The film showing at The Picture House was the controversial *The Outlaw*, in which Howard Hughes, eccentric and rich, featured his protégé, Jane Russell. It was made in 1943, but the censor considered that the War and its aftermath was enough for the world to cope with and Miss Russell's charms could wait. The film was finally shown in Paisley around June 1948.

A good view of the High Street looking west, featuring The Picture House, The Shoe Corner and a terrace of magnificent buildings and shopfronts. See the lady decorously leaving the car, with its door sensibly opening backwards. Pedestrianisation (an ugly word) has a lot to answer for.

HIGH STREET, PAISLEY.   D.1794

The photographer's work has been spoiled by clumsy retouching here – is that blob in the distance meant to be the Coats Memorial? It looks more like the Rock of Gibraltar. Many of the shops can be identified. The City Bakeries Tea Rooms, Marks and Spencer and The Picture House, with restaurant, are on the left. On the right are R. S. McColl's, Macduff & Co., F. W. Woolworth's, A. L. Scott's and Cable. Showing at the cinema was *Top Banana*, starring Phil Silvers, released in 1953 and dating the scene to then or 1954.

No, this isn't St Mirren's latest signing upon their return to the Big Time. Mind you, four of those on the goal line might keep out the Old Firm sharpshooters. The budding keeper is seen at the racecourse. The circus used to be a regular visitor to Paisley (until political correctness caught up with it) and I can recall seeing the parade going along Caledonia Street. One resident, John McIntyre, called to his mother to come and see the horse tethered outside the pub across the road (its cowboy rider was inside for a drink). She didn't believe him.

This good-looking group formed the Bobby Barr Dancers. Mr Barr had a dance studio in the High Street and no less a personality than Mr Paisley, David Rowand, let slip that he had taken lessons there. As the song went, 'Arthur Murray taught me to dance in a hurry'. Paisley's answer to the famous American dance school was very popular. The blonde dancer standing up is Bonnie Barr, Mr Barr's daughter. The seated blonde has landed herself an American (note the inverted chevrons on his sleeve; perhaps he was from the Polaris base). Anyway, it's unlikely that he sent a copy of this home to his mum.

The quizzical Mr MacDonald, of the Gleniffer Press, with a selection of his popular mini books, one of which – possibly the one in the case on the right – is listed in the *Guinness Book of Records* as the smallest book ever printed. He now runs his business in the book town of Wigtown.

Annie Brown organised the Buddies Club holiday programme and other events. Here she is, standing in front of Concorde, on its first visit to Abbotsinch (believed to be about 1971). Following the Paris disaster a decision on the future of Concorde is awaited.

We have all heard
of having designs
on someone, but
this is ridiculous.
The illustrated
man – shades of
Ray Bradbury
and Rod Steiger –
appears to date
from the 1950s
and, I was told
came from
Ferguslie.
Someone is sure
to remember him,
his family or the
person who
created this
mobile art-form,
so write and let us
know.

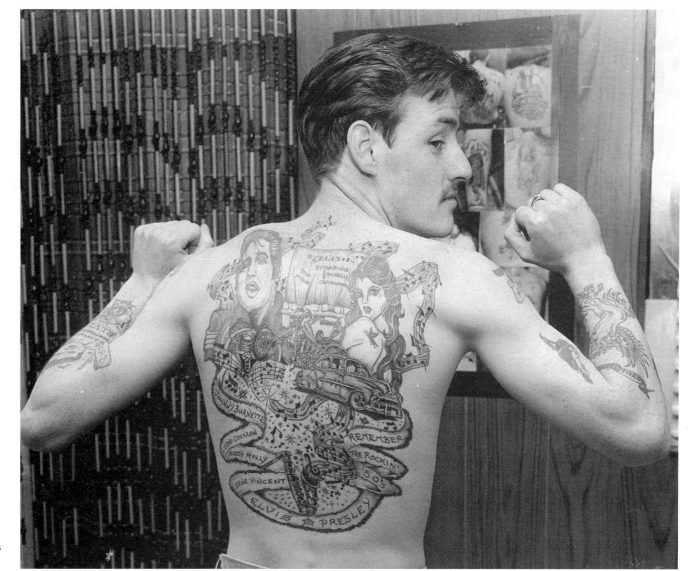

21

'George Dobie & Son Ltd., Paisley, Scotland. Manufacturers of Quality Tobaccos since 1809.' Thus runs the legend on this famous company's products. Latterly located at Greenhill Road, Dobie's was a major employer in the town, and is one of many important firms that have disappeared from the local economy. Dobie's was world-famous for its Four Square products, the logo appearing in various colours. I have a tin (cigarettes), a 20 packet and 1 oz of matured Virginia tobacco in a wartime wrapper (tin plate was scarce at the time).

A story is told of a sergeant who was shot down over Nürnberg during the War. Having parachuted to safety, the first thing he did was to lean against a tree and take out his Dobie's Four Square. This bustling photograph shows packing cases full of tobacco tins, along with batteries of scales where the staff presumably weighed and packed the tobacco.

In February 1952 the great Scottish actor and comedian Duncan Macrae visited Dobie's. The vivacious young lady was Julie Lang, the Belle of the Ball, so he was probably there for a presentation.

Not surprisingly, Duncan Macrae's presence at Dobie's drew a crowd. He's seen here signing autographs for some admirers, several of whom I recognise, including Julie (featured opposite).

This intrepid trio is out on the Clyde – that looks like Greenock in the background – asserting Renfrewshire's river rights, an annual occasion. A perusal of several Paisley volumes reveals no direct reference to such a ceremony, although Frederick Mort, in *Cambridge County Geographies – Renfrewshire*, 1912, reminds us that 'We are apt to forget that for a short distance – between Whiteinch and Yoker – the Clyde is purely a Renfrewshire river'. The ceremony has a solemn ring to it, but evidently had become a light-hearted event by the time this picture was taken. The man on the left is unidentified; Councillor William Darroch and George Logie (who was provost from 1980 to 1984) complete the group.

The Queen and Prince Philip visited Paisley on 25 June 1953, arriving at Gilmour Street station at 11.05 a.m., where they were greeted by the band of HMS *Sanderling*. Provost C. Stewart Black and Town Clerk Morrison (seen here), along with other local worthies, were presented to Her Majesty at a ceremony held on a dais in front of the Municipal Buildings, in which she signed the visitors' book. According to the *Paisley Daily Express*, the Queen wore an ink-blue paper silk dress, white straw hat, white shoes and gloves. Her jewellery comprised pearl-stud earrings, a diamond lapel clip and pearls. This, the first of many trips to the town, had its amusing aspect. The station had been repainted – but only the parts that the Queen might see – with the rest of the building left its old sooty, grimy self.

The Paisley Rocketeers Society was formed in 1936 by John D. Stewart. The years until 1939 were filled with experiments, most of them successful and all meticulously recorded. Dissolved on the outbreak of war, the society was reconstituted in 1965 upon the suggestion of Mrs Margaret Morris (née Watson), a philatelist of international repute – the society not only launches rockets, but produces highly collectable rocket mail too. The picture was taken at the launching of RR-62 on the Gleniffer Braes, 27 November 1965. Left to right are Margaret Watson, Donald Malcolm, Gordon Malcolm, John Armour, John Stewart, Rita Malcolm and Dr A. E. Roy. The Society's 65th anniversary falls in 2001, the true millennium date.

The site of the Fountain Gardens was originally purchased by John Love – hence Love Street – and developed by him as Hope Temple Gardens. After his South American interests received a setback Thomas Coats bought the area and presented it to the town in 1866. On 26 May 1868, Queen Victoria's birthday, the Fountain Gardens were officially opened. The fountain, with its four walruses, was the work of George Smith & Co., Sun Foundry, Glasgow, and was designed by F. W. Pomeroy. There are identical statues in Sydney, Australia and Auckland, New Zealand. The fountain was working when this photograph was taken, although it has been dry for a long time now.

FOUNTAIN GARDENS, PAISLEY D 3750

Macdonald's Rest was built in 1900 by the grandfather of Paisley resident, Ian Pollock. In 1911, a tearoom was opened and the last person in the family to own it was Miss Pollock (Ian's aunt), who sold it to a Glasgow firm in 1948 or 1949. A Mr Wingate of Renfrew ran the business until around 1959, when it closed. After a time, it passed to James Mackie, Potato Merchant. Eventually it was demolished, probably in the mid-1960s. Mr Mackie's next venture in the vicinity was a proposed hotel, which fell foul of planning regulations and the derelict hulk of the building has been a blot on the landscape for over 25 years. According to a newspaper report of 28 September this year the present owner, John Hadden, has been instructed to demolish the building and restore the site, otherwise Renfrewshire Council will do so and send him the bill. As a postscript to the Pollock family, it is interesting to note that Ian Pollock is a descendent of the poet Tannahill's mother, who was Jane Pollock of Kilmaurs.

MACDONALD'S REST, GLENIFFER BRAES, PAISLEY. 1155

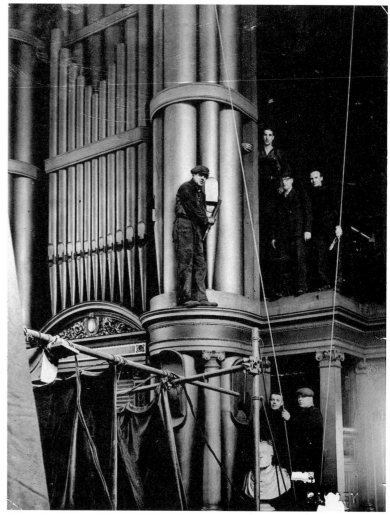

Camphill Secondary School had two murals. The one in the refectory, based on fairy tales and cartoon figures, was designed and painted by Bill Baillie, Tom Gibson, Jessie Matthews and Helen Elder. The work was done after the 1947 Highers and Bill relates that the girls neatly solved the problem of propriety posed by ladders by turning up in trousers, something that no school countenanced in those days. Bill is seen here working on Peter and the Wolf. The art teacher was J. D. Cruikshank. Bill and Tom both went on to train as architects, one with David Murray, the other with Davidson, both firms in Paisley.

The organ in the Town Hall is undergoing repair and renovation in this scene. That must be the gaffer in the suit and soft hat. Research hasn't revealed a date for the picture, although some time in the 1950s seems likely.

BOOK-JACKET FOR "THE LAST OF THE MOHICANS"

THE
LAST
OF THE
MOHICANS

DONALD MALCOLM   CLASS 5C

PAISLEY LIBRARY AND MUSEUM.

Children's Art Competition.

2nd PRIZE

No. 825

Name, *Donald Malcolm* Age 16
School, *Camphill Secondary*
Private Address *17 Caledonia St.*
Previous Success(es), *None* 19
I certify that the above particulars are correct.
S. D. Cruickshank Teacher.

This portion to be sealed in numbered envelope.

BURGH OF PAISLEY

PUBLIC LIBRARY, MUSEUM AND ART GALLERIES

SCHOOL CHILDREN'S ART COMPETITIONS

This is to Certify that, in the Competitions
promoted by the Committee of Management of
the Public Library, Museum and Art Galleries,
the Adjudicators awarded this

Certificate of Merit

to

DONALD MALCOLM

Section, Special -
        Book Jacket.
Adjudicators: Wm. Hunter, S.D.I.,
        Ian Fleming, A.R.S.A.

Paisley, December, 1947.

The school children's art competitions were very popular in Paisley. I entered in the Special Section, Book Jacket and chose James Fenimore Cooper's famous story, *The Last of the Mohicans* (although who ever heard of a book jacket without the writer's name!). There was a strange outcome to my entry, which reflected the social climate of the time, 1947. My entry was judged to be the winner. But the adjudicators decided that it was 'too advanced' for the age group (up to 16), and the first prize was awarded to the runner-up instead. That was accepted without protest: authority couldn't be challenged in those days and I lost the prize.

The diligent little boy, the important focus of the picture, is unnamed, while a Mr Dunn, whose group this was, is recorded for posterity. Maybe someone will recognise the lad, who is drawing his impression of a mammoth in pastels, *c*.1959.

A busy group of children in the Junior Museum Club, engaged in drawing, reading or simply mooning the time away – look at some of those expressions! The club met on Saturday mornings in the museum's general section.

The children's art competitions, sponsored by the local museum, are long-established, maintaining and strengthening the interest of young people in the arts. Most of the participants went on to follow other careers, but many subsequently recalled their time spent drawing and painting in the competitions and clubs. Encouragement of an enduring interest in the arts is a cornerstone of civilisation. This picture dates from 1949 or 1950.

A bunch of happy flag-wavers, not understanding very much about the Coronation, but delighted to have a day off school, and a sunny one at that.

The Coronation Pageant, 6 June 1953, is passing the museum, which supplied some of the dresses worn in the stagecoach. Arthur's the Jewellers, where my wife and I bought our wedding rings, was the last shop in the tenement (the dark building). All the premises to the right were eventually demolished and the university now occupies the site. The former Regal Cinema is out of sight, beyond the tramcar. About midway along this stretch was the British Restaurant, for which the Burgh of Paisley issued undenominated plastic tokens. These restaurants were set up during the War by the Government to ensure that good food was widely available at reasonable prices.

THE CROSS AND HIGH STREET, PAISLEY

D 3746

A cracking piece of photography and a splendid skyline. A magnifying glass reveals the traffic packing the High Street. There were the usual complaints about congestion and pollution, but, with the street's closure, these have simply been shunted elsewhere and the area has lost a dimension that gave it vibrancy. Now the High Street is like a wake without the humour, and the traffic policeman, with his white coat, has been made redundant.

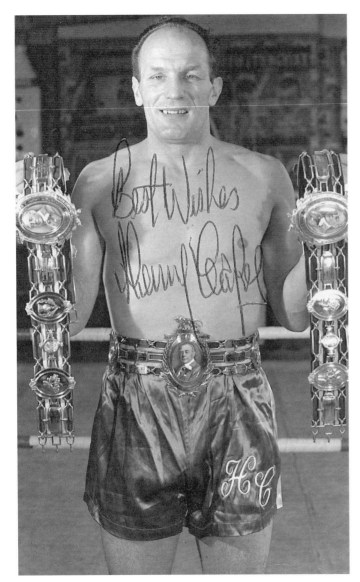

This is a different kind of punch-line from that normally associated with British heavyweight champion Henry Cooper, holder of three Lonsdale belts. He's at Woolworth's in the High Street, plugging Brut by Faberge, and he's obviously a big hit with the onlookers.

Norman Buchan, MP, John Carty, a union representative, Tommy Graham, Allan Adams (both became MPs) and a mystery man, probably photographed during an election campaign.

Like the last soldier to fall in battle, this leviathan at Ferguslie Mills begins its collapse, becoming an ignominious pile of bricks amid the rubble of what was once a great global thread empire. Many working lives, particularly those of women, were spent here. The Counting House escaped destruction and was converted into flats as part of a private housing development on the site in January 1984.

Many traditional crafts and trades have been lost over the years, but basket making for a commercial concern must have been one of the more unusual ones. William Wright Gray was apprenticed to his father for five years at Ferguslie Mills. Five men worked under Mr Gray senior in the basement of the Experimental Mill. By the time his son took over, he was on his own and working on a part-time basis. He made and repaired the stock of about 3,000 baskets used in the spinning and twisting departments. Cane was imported from Japan and Borneo (although in wartime English willow was used). The pictures date from June 1961.

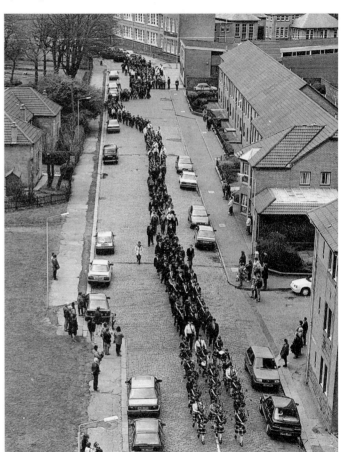

Left: Unfortunately, there are no details to identify with certainty this dramatic picture. However, the protesting woman seems to be at the gatehouse of the Rootes car factory, Linwood – to judge by the placard, at the time of its closure in the mid-1970s.

Paisley and parades go together. This one is leaving the West School (long since gone) – Maxwellton Park is on the left – and appears to be of the Boys Brigade and perhaps other youth organisations.

Paisley has a proud radical past, with its citizens never being slow to acknowledge their obligations or to enforce their privileges. The car industry at Linwood had a troubled history of employer-worker relations and strikes were frequent. In this picture the Talbot Joint Stewards Committee and the Transport and General Workers Union are prominent as the workers air a grievance at the junction of William Street and Broomlands.

Wages and conditions have been long-running bones of contention in the nursing profession and occasionally members take to the barricades, as this resolute group of Dykebar nurses have done. They were supported by Norman Buchan and Allan Adams. Such action takes on a new resonance with the proposal to locate patients in a high-risk category at the hospital.

The rubbish piles up during a pay and conditions protest at Underwood Road Cleansing Department, which was located on this site in 1900. People with cars tended to bring their bags to join the pile, but not everyone had access to transport and Paisley was not a pretty sight at the time, with refuse stacked up everywhere.

The scene is County Square, the date 1 September 1969 and the occasion an anti-rent increase demonstration, convened by the Paisley Council of Tenants' Associations. The Chairman was William McQuilkin. Amongst the large crowd, I can pick out my wife, standing towards the left of the group.

44

Bobby Borland and his sister inherited a light removals business from their father and much of the work involved transporting and delivering goods from auction rooms. Here they are in Inchinnan Road (not far from the Love Street end of St Mirren Park), where a wooden bedstead end is being loaded aboard while the transaction is diligently recorded and the pony waits patiently. The factory in the background was occupied by various firms over the years, including Ronald, Jack & Co. Ltd., which was in the carpet trade before it merged with Stoddard of Elderslie. When this picture was annotated in 1978 the premises were being used by a wholesale furniture firm. One thing was certain: Bobby and his sister never had to worry about a petrol shortage.

Much has changed in the fifty years since this famous picture was taken in 1953. The tram, no. 190, is turning into Gilmour Street which, along with part of the High Street, is now closed to traffic. Its destination was Renfrew Ferry. Together with all the other cinemas in Paisley, La Scala has long gone, the site now occupied by Littlewoods. All the premises on the same side as the cinema, such as the Maypole Dairy and the City Bakeries, have changed occupancy. Note the British Oxygen Company lorry behind the tram. La Scala had what must have been an advanced sound system, advertised on the building. For more on the history of all forms of wheeled transport in the town, see *Wheels Around Paisley* by Robert Grieves, published by and available from Stenlake Publishing.

A relaxed driver on the footplate of a BR Standard Class 4, 2-6-4T engine at Gilmour Street station, probably heading for Largs. The photograph was taken on 30 April 1965.